This Books Belongs To.........

....

....

....

Trace the steps for making the letter a on the following line.

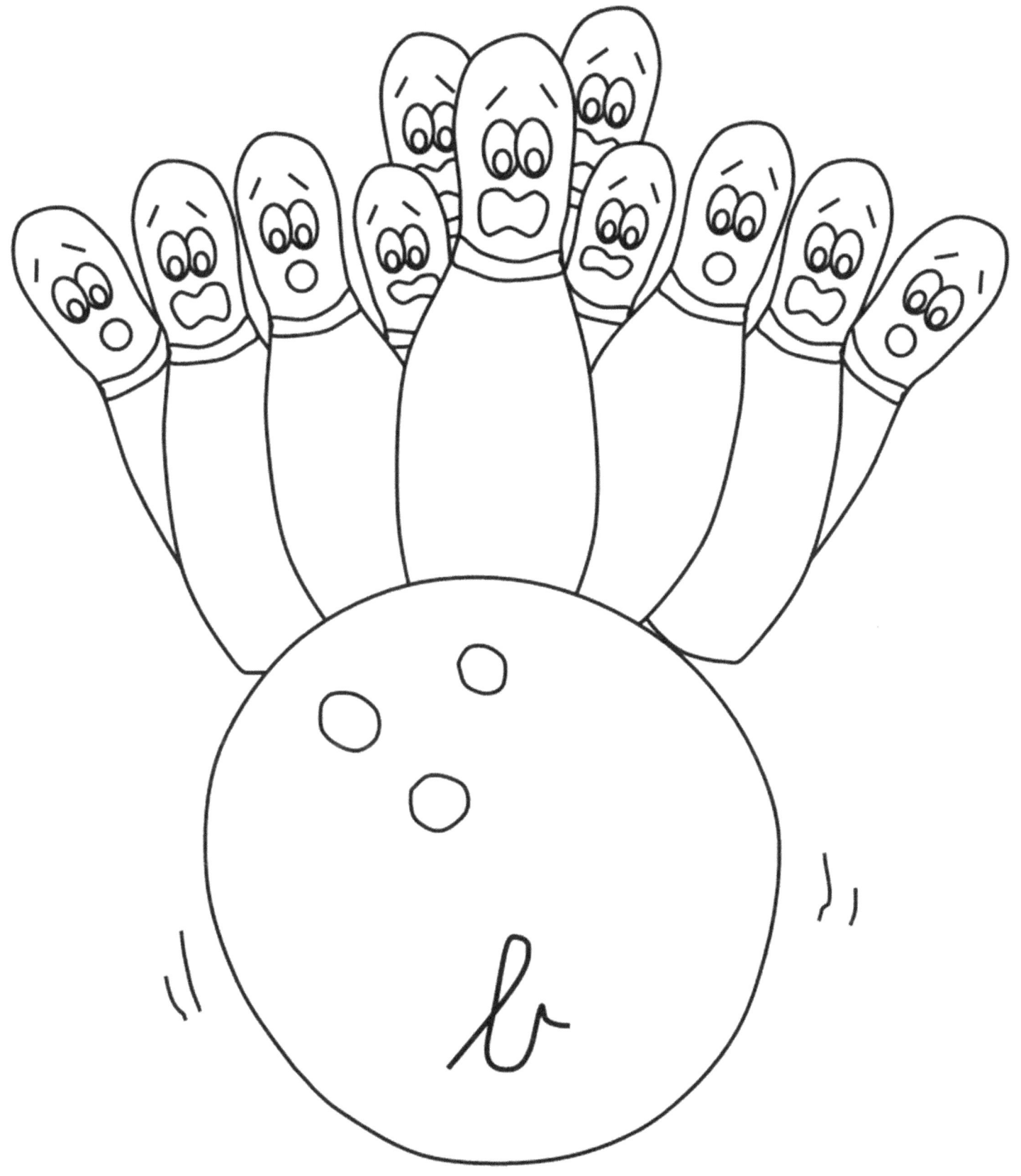

Trace the steps for making the letter b on the following line.

Trace the steps for making the letter c on the following line.

Trace the steps for making the letter c on the following line.

_c_ _h_ _ch_ _ch_ _ch_

Trace the steps for making the letter d on the following line.

_ _

Trace the steps for making the letter e on the following line.

Trace the steps for making the letter f on the following line.

Trace the steps for making the letter g on the following line.

Trace the steps for making the letter h on the following line.

Trace the steps for making the letter i on the following line.

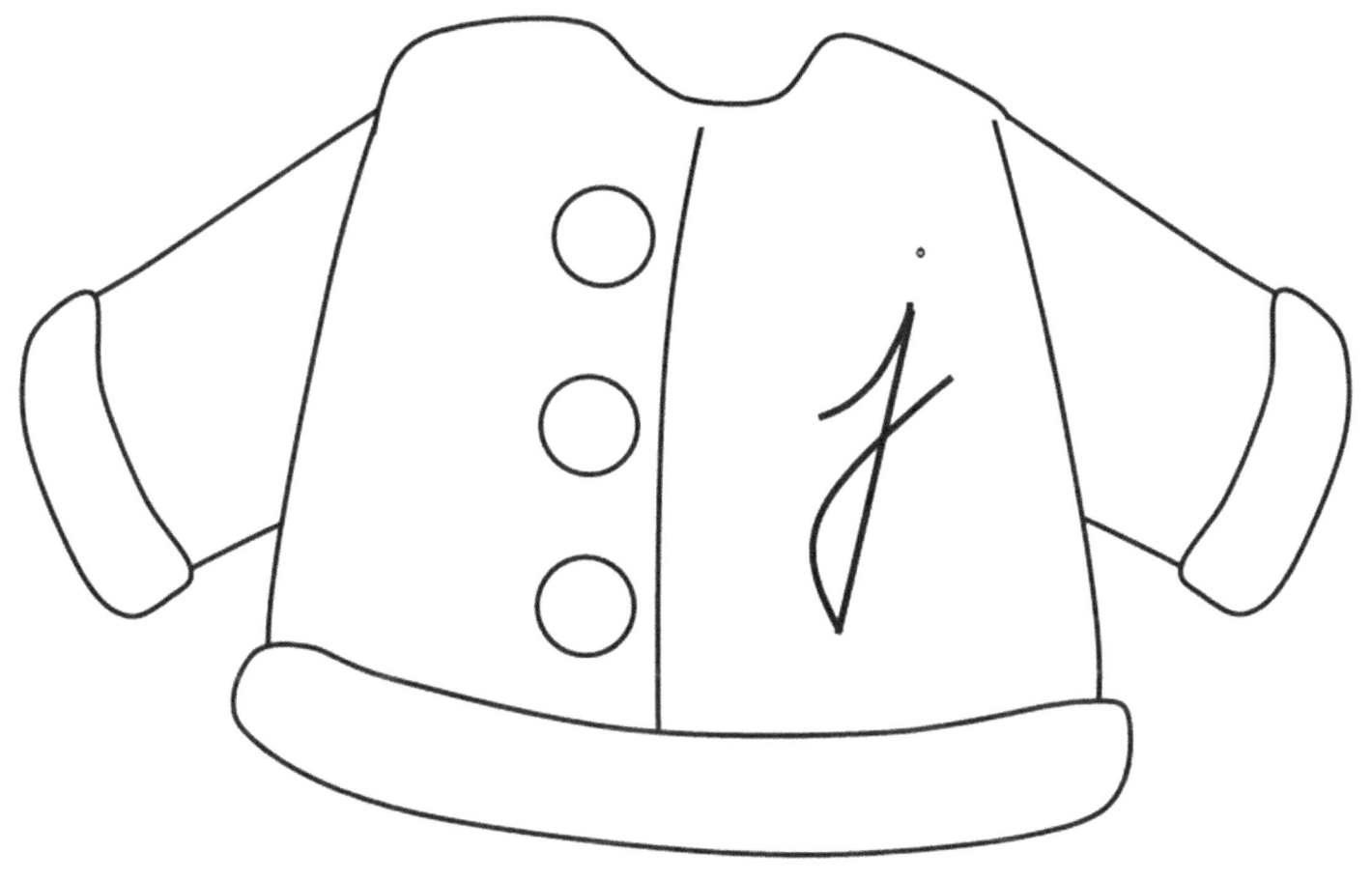

Trace the steps for making the letter j on the following line.

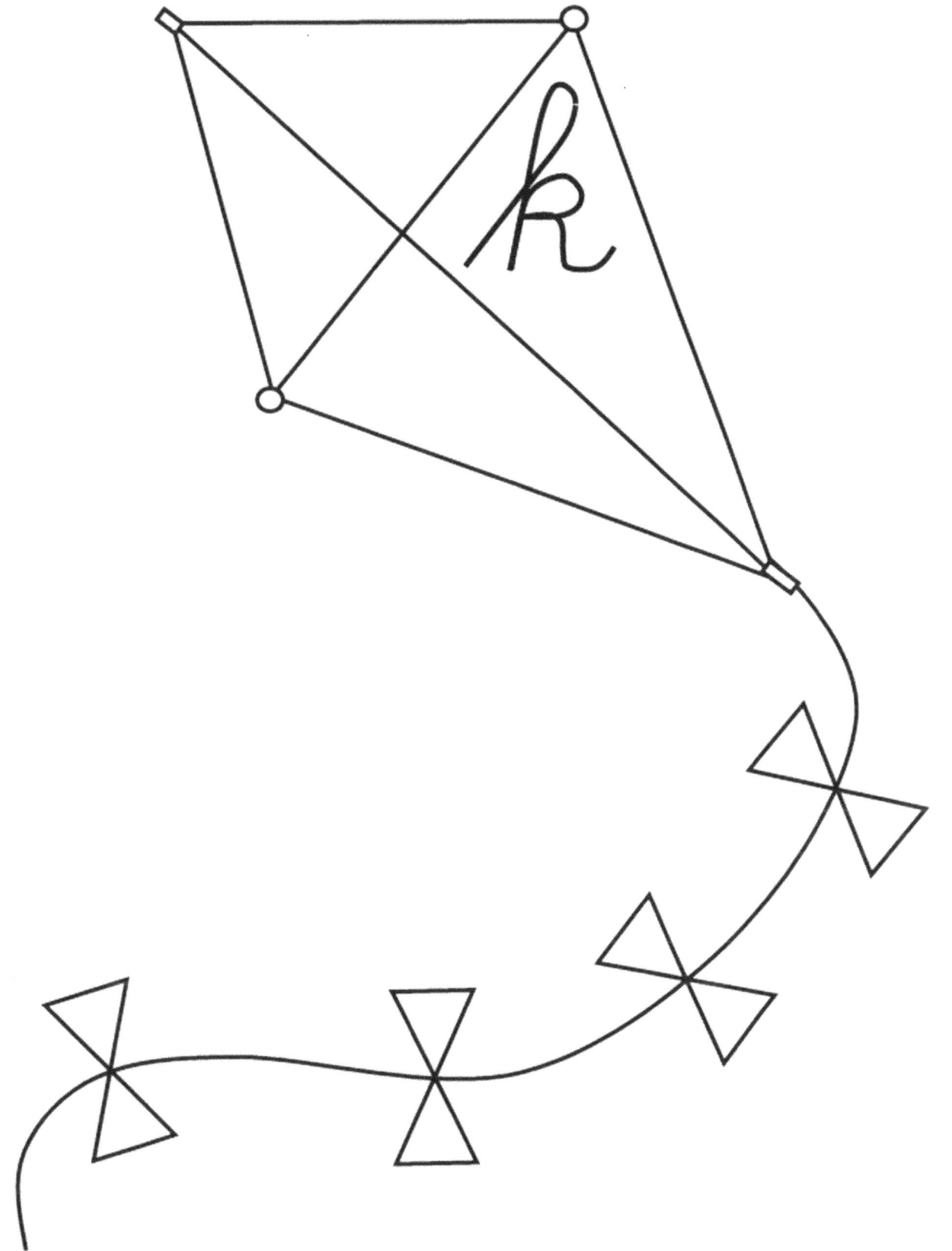

Trace the steps for making the letter k on the following line.

Trace the steps for making the letter l on the following line.

Trace the steps for making the letter m on the following line.

_____

m   m   m   m   m   m   m   m

Trace the steps for making the letter n on the following line.

Trace the steps for making the letter o on the following line.

Trace the steps for making the letter p on the following line.

Trace the steps for making the letter q on the following line.

Trace the steps for making the letter r on the following line.

Trace the steps for making the letter s on the following line.

Trace the steps for making the letter sh on the following line.

_s_ _h_ _sh_ _sh_ _sh_ _sh_

Trace the steps for making the letter t on the following line.

Trace the steps for making the letter th on the following line.

th   th   th   th   th

Trace the steps for making the letter u on the following line.

Trace the steps for making the letter v on the following line.

Trace the steps for making the letter w on the following line.

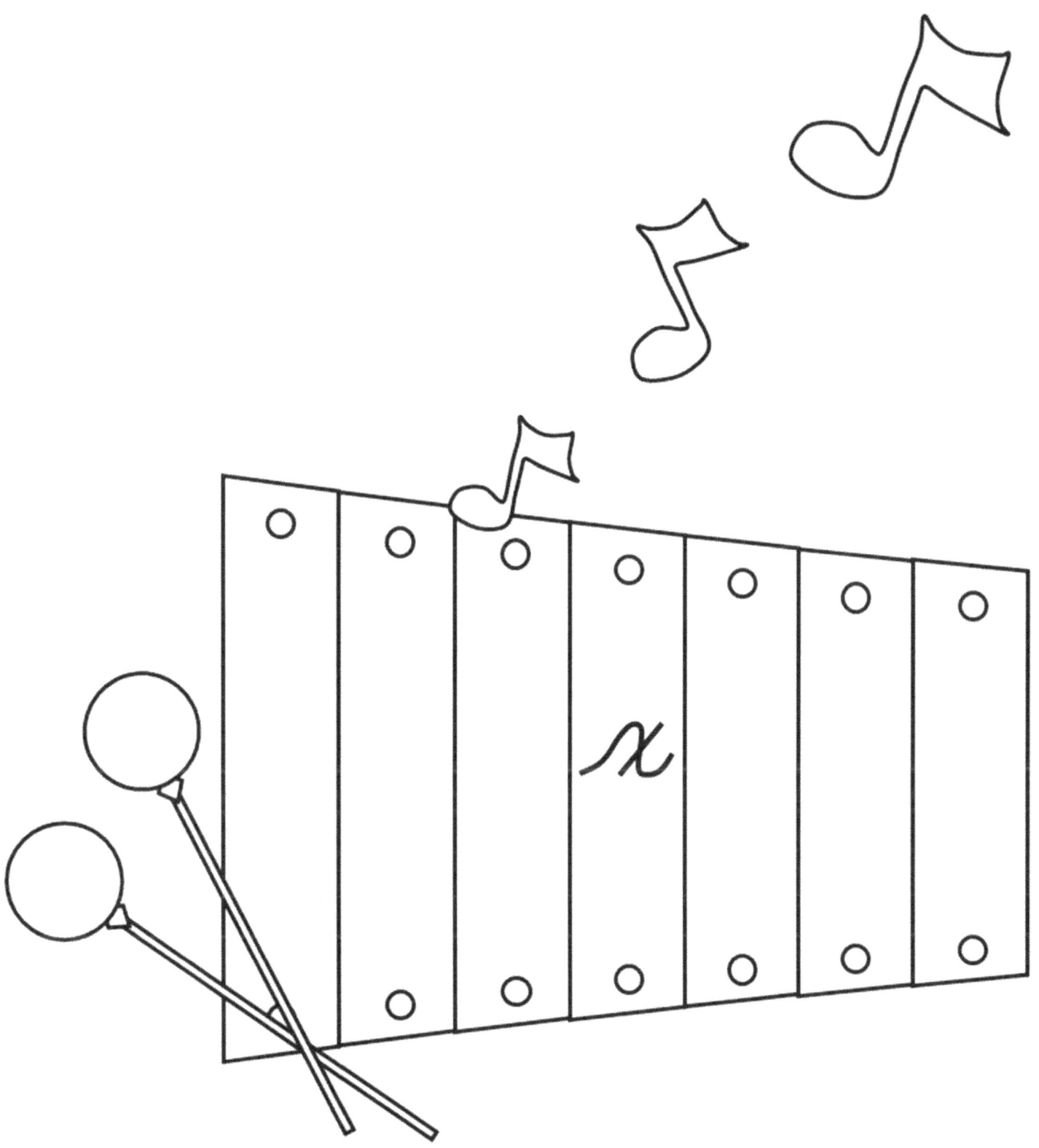

Trace the steps for making the letter x on the following line.

Trace the steps for making the letter y on the following line.

Trace the steps for making the letter z on the following line.